WITHDRAWN

GULLS

Tom Jackson

Grolier
an imprint of
SCHOLASTIC
www.scholastic.com/librarypublishing

Published 2008 by Grolier
An imprint of Scholastic Library Publishing
Old Sherman Turnpike, Danbury,
Connecticut 06816

For The Brown Reference Group plc
Project Editor: Jolyon Goddard
Copy-editors: Lesley Ellis, Lisa Hughes,
    Wendy Horobin
Picture Researcher: Clare Newman
Designers: Jeni Child, Lynne Ross,
    Sarah Williams
Managing Editor: Bridget Giles

Volume ISBN-13: 978-0-7172-6256-4
Volume ISBN-10: 0-7172-6256-1

**Library of Congress
Cataloging-in-Publication Data**

Nature's children. Set 2.
    p. cm.
    Includes bibliographical references and
index.
    ISBN-13: 978-0-7172-8081-0
    ISBN-10: 0-7172-8081-0
    1. Animals--Encyclopedias, Juvenile. I.
Grolier (Firm)
    QL49.N383 2007
    590--dc22
                            2007026928

Printed and bound in China

PICTURE CREDITS

Front Cover: **Shutterstock**: Michael
Ransburg

Back Cover: **Shutterstock**: Baudot, Karl R.
Martin, Sean Nel, Yoka Van Eekelen

Alamy: Renee Morris 18; **Corbis**: Roger
Tidman 17, Martin B. Withers/FLPA 45;
FLPA: Michael Fogden 14; **Nature PL**:
George McCarthy 42, Artur Tabor 34;
NHPA: Louis Le Moigne 9; **Photos.com**:
41; **Shutterstock**: Maksym Gorpenyuk 33,
Gail Johnson 13, Milan M. Jurkovic 2–3, 22,
Heather Lewis 29, Chris Loneragan 6,
Bruce MacQueen 30, Sean Nel 5, Svetlana
Privezentseva 46, Richard Thornton 4, TT
Photo 10, Paul S. Wolf 21; **Still Pictures**: C.
Allan Morgan 38, Tom Vezo 37, C. Wermter
26–27.

Contents

FACT FILE: Gulls

Class	Birds (Aves)
Order	Plovers, sandpipers, gulls, terns, and auks (Charadriiformes)
Family	Gulls and terns (Laridae)
Genus	*Larus*
Species	More than 40 species, 26 of which live in North America
World distribution	Gulls live around the coasts of all parts of the world
Habitat	Live in or near to water in all climates
Distinctive physical characteristics	Gray and white plumage, with a large, hooked beak; webbed feet; legs and beak are often yellow
Habits	Gulls usually live in colonies; they lay three eggs at a time; males and females mate for life; they both sit on the nest; many northern gulls migrate south for winter
Diet	Fish, crustaceans, and squid

Introduction

When you stand next to the ocean, there are two sounds that you can't fail to hear. One is the roar of the waves crashing onto the shore. The other sound is the screeching of gulls. The gulls are everywhere, soaring gracefully through the air, bobbing on the surface of the water, perching on the cliffs, or strutting along the beach.

Seagulls are fascinating birds. Some fly across oceans, while others live on beaches. Gulls are often mischief-makers, crowding around picnics to snatch food scraps. But they don't live just by the oceans—you'll also find them in huge numbers inland, in cities, on rivers, and by lakes.

A cape gull settles on a sandy beach.

A seagull stands on a rock. All gulls have large, webbed feet.

Not the Same

There are more than 40 species, or types, of gulls in the world. Each one has something that makes it different from the others, although most of them do look very similar. Most gulls have a white body with gray wings. Some have a black head, although most have a white one. A gull's beak, or bill, is long and curves down at the tip. Most gulls have a yellow or black beak. Many seagull beaks have bright red spots on them.

The birds' legs are also brightly colored. They may be gray, black, orange, or even pink! Seagulls are waterbirds and their feet are webbed. The skin stretches between their toes to make a wide paddle, which is perfect for swimming.

Great and Small

Different species of seagulls look very much alike. So how can you tell them apart? One way is to look at where they live. The western gull lives along the western coast of North America. Some gulls do not live by the sea. For example, Franklin's gull lives in the marshy prairies of the northern United States and southern Canada.

The smallest gull is called the little gull, and it is just 11 inches (28 cm) long from head to tail. The great black-backed gull is a giant; it is 29 inches (74 cm) long. As you can see, the names of many different gull species also give you a clue as to what they look like.

A great black-backed gull balances on some rocks.

9

Gulls follow a plowing tractor.

Mass Gatherings

Gulls are not difficult to see in the wild. You are most likely to come across them by the ocean, but these birds come inland, too. Some gulls travel far up rivers. Others make their home around large lakes. Some cities are filled with gulls. There they raid garbage bins, peck at litter on the street, and nest among the chimneys.

Wherever you see one gull, you will probably see many more. They like to live in large groups, called flocks. Some flocks might contain more than 100 thousand birds! These large groups are called **colonies**. A colony often breaks up into smaller groups. Most gulls will stay in their group for their whole life.

Your Tern?

Gulls are not the only seabirds to crowd together into large colonies. They have close relatives, called terns, which do the same. A colony of gulls often lives next door to a group of terns. Both gulls and terns tend to be gray and white. Some have black patches as well. So how can you tell the difference between the two types of birds? Terns are usually smaller than gulls. They are also much more acrobatic fliers. While gulls soar for hours on the wind only flapping occasionally, terns twist and turn at great speed. The birds have different shaped tails that help them fly like that. Gulls have a wide, fan-shaped tail, while terns have a forked tail. Terns also fly with their head facing down, looking at the water. Gulls keep looking straight forward for most of the time.

An arctic tern
prepares to attack.

Using its beak, a young black-backed gull preens its feathers.

Oiling the Feathers

The surface of the sea can get rough at times, with the wind whipping spray high into the air. It seems likely then that seagulls would get drenched several times a day. However, just as a deep-sea fisher keeps dry under waterproof clothes, a gull keeps dry with waterproof feathers. Each feather is coated in a thin layer of oil. The water runs off the oily layer, unable to soak into the feathers. The oil comes from a **gland** positioned under the gull's tail. The bird uses its beak to spread the oil over its feathers.

Gulls must also keep their feathers clean so they can fly properly. Several times each day they take a moment to rearrange their ruffled feathers. This process is called **preening**. It is very important that their feathers stay waterproof and straight. In fact, gulls learn that at a very young age. Gulls start preening before they can fly or even stand up!

Falling Feathers!

Despite all the oiling and preening, a gull's feathers still get damaged from time to time. After a while, the feathers become too tattered to work properly and must be replaced. Gulls replace all their feathers twice a year in a process called **molting**. The birds molt in spring and then again in fall. During a molt, the old feathers fall out and new ones grow in their place.

The molt takes a few weeks. The feathers fall out gradually, one by one, and the gull can still fly during this time. If all the feathers fell out at the same time, the gull would be unable to fly, as well as bald and cold! **Predators** that prey on gulls would also find it much easier to attack the birds if they were unable to take flight. However, when some other types of seabirds molt, they cannot fly and therefore have to take great care avoiding their enemies.

A common gull rests on a beach while it molts. Its normally smooth feathers are untidy and ragged.

A laughing gull perches on the head of a brown pelican, waiting for the chance to snatch fish from the larger bird's mouth.

Winged Robbers

Gulls are the thieves of the bird world. They are just as happy to steal another bird's food as they are to find their own. Gulls are such skilled robbers that they can snatch food right out of the mouth of another bird. Once a gull has some food, it does not give it up without a fight. Therefore, gulls of the same species do not usually steal from one another—it would simply be too tiring. Instead, gulls swoop in on other birds that cannot defend themselves. If a gull cannot snatch the food directly, it jostles the other bird until it drops the food in fright.

Anything to Eat?

Gulls never get very hungry. That is because they will eat just about anything—fish, worms, seeds, insects, and even dead animals and garbage! If it can be swallowed, a gull will eat it. Seagulls are most fond of seafood, including fish, **shellfish**, and starfish. They snatch fish from the the surface of the water. But they have to work even harder to enjoy a meal of shellfish. They must crack open a clam or oyster shell before they can eat the soft flesh inside. The gulls carry the shell into the air and drop it onto hard rocks below. It might take several trips before the shell finally cracks, but it's worth it!

A seagull is trying to swallow a large starfish that it has found on the beach.

A colony of
breeding seagulls
shares nesting space
on a rocky cliff.

Forming a Colony

Gulls lay their eggs in spring. That way the chicks hatch in summer when the weather is good and their parents can find plenty of food for them. Most gulls nest on a beach or a coastal cliff. As with everything else they do, gulls do not nest on their own. The first bird to arrive at the nesting site is not alone for long. Hundreds of gulls arrive every day. Within a few weeks, the place is alive with many thousands of birds.

Nesting together is a defense tactic. Any predators that choose to attack will be easily spotted by one of the many gulls. The gulls work together to chase away their enemy. A few unlucky birds are still killed. But with so many birds in one place, the chances of a predator getting close enough to attack are very low.

Pairing Up

The first thing gulls do after arriving at a colony is find a **mate**. Males choose a place on the beach or cliff and wait for a female gull to come calling. The female circles above her chosen male and tosses her head about as she calls to him. He replies by calling back and tugging at the grass and twigs around him. The female then lands next to him and demands to be fed by the male.

A pair of gulls repeats this ritual many times to build up a strong bond. The pair will then mate for life. Although the male and female spend winter alone, they will come back to the same colony the following spring and seek out their mate among the crowd.

Setting Up Home

Choosing a good nesting site is an important decision for gulls. Each pair prefers to be in the middle of the colony, where predators cannot reach them. The competition for space is fierce. Once a pair has selected a spot, they must take turns guarding their new home from other pairs of gulls who might try to steal it.

Intruders are ordered to stay away by the nesting birds. The gulls throw back their head and give out loud trumpeting noises as a warning to others to keep their distance. After days of squabbling, the colony eventually quiets down. Each pair of gulls has found a place to nest. They also have learned to stop trespassing in one another's area.

A couple of black-headed gulls nuzzle their beaks as they get to know each other.

Making the Nest

Gulls do not build complicated nests. They simply choose a flat ledge or an area of sand that is protected by surrounding rocks or thickets of grass. The gulls then clear away any stones and scratch a hole into the ground (if it is soft enough). They complete their nest by lining it with soft leaves, seaweed, and twigs.

The nest is now ready for the eggs. A female gull normally lays three eggs. They are usually all the same size, but often have slightly different colors. The colors are never bright, but dull shades of gray, olive green, or pale brown. The eggs are generally covered in dark blotches, which make them harder to see from above. That keeps the eggs safe from circling crows and other enemies.

Three speckled seagull eggs lie safely in a nest.

29

A black-backed jackal
has caught and killed
a kelp gull.

Enemies Close

Gulls work together to ensure that foxes, eagles, and other predators do not get into the colony to eat the eggs and chicks. As soon as a gull spots an intruder, it lets out a warning call to its neighbors. Soon a crowd of gulls swoops around the attacker, snapping at it with their beaks and beating it with their wings. The intruder will be lucky to snatch one chick and make its escape.

While a colony of gulls can easily protect themselves, it is much harder for a pair of gulls to defend their chicks against their most dangerous enemies—neighboring gulls. While gull parents work hard to protect their own young, they will happily **prey** on and eat the chicks of the seagulls nesting next door.

Brooding Pair

After the eggs are laid, a pair of gulls takes turns protecting their eggs. There is always one parent at the nest. The gull sits on the eggs to keep them safe, but also to keep them warm so the chicks continue to grow inside. The parent birds often quarrel about whose turn it is to **brood**, or care for, the eggs.

Each bird has three bare patches on its underside—one for each egg. Each egg rests against a patch, touching the parent bird's warm skin. In this way, the eggs are kept at just the right temperature. On warm days, the parents do not sit on the eggs. They stand to the side, keeping their precious eggs shaded from the hot sun.

A seagull stands above its eggs, shielding them from the heat of the sun.

Using the egg tooth at the end of its beak, a black-headed gull chick hatches from its egg.

Hatching Out

The eggs are brooded for around 25 days.
It is then time for the chicks to hatch. Before
hatching, the chicks start making tiny squeaking
sounds from inside the egg. Shortly after the
first squeak is heard, a crack appears at one end
of the shell. Inside, the chick is using a pointed
egg tooth that sticks out of the top of its beak to
crack through the eggshell. It might take the
chick all day to make a hole large enough for
it to get through, but eventually it is out. After
all that effort, the chick is too tired to move.
It lies in the nest, still wet from the contents
of the egg, and gathers its strength.

Fluffy Chick

Once its feathers have dried out, a newly
hatched chick appears to have doubled in size!
The soft, fluffy feathers, known as **down**, stick
out in all directions. The downy feathers are
no good for flying—the chick is too young and
weak to fly anyway. Instead, the down keeps
the young gull warm. People often use down
feathers for the same reason. They use the down
from larger birds, such as ducks, to stuff quilts
and coats.

Within a few days, all the chicks in the nest
will have hatched. The parents ensure that the
broken shells are thrown away. The eggs are
camouflaged on the outside. But inside they
are bright white. These white interiors alert
predators that newly hatched chicks are close by.

A fluffy, newly hatched herring gull chick stands beside its broken eggshell.

By tapping the parent's beak, a Heermann's gull chick encourages the adult to cough up food for it.

Cough Up Now

Baby chicks can do only two things: eat and sleep. They do not sleep for long, however. After a couple of hours, they are hungry again. Their parents take turns finding food for the babies. Once they've found a tasty snack, the adult gull does not carry it home but swallows it itself! When the adult gets home, one of the chicks taps its parent on the red spot on its beak. This action prompts the adult gull to cough up the food it has recently swallowed. Carefully, the parent bird puts the food into the chick's mouth.

Within a few days, the chick grows strong enough to feed itself. But the young bird has to be quick—otherwise its brothers and sisters will get it first.

Growing Up

Newly hatched chicks are too weak to stand. But the young birds become better at balancing on two feet as they grow. Before long, they are eagerly scrambling out of the nest and exploring the wide world beyond. However, the parents do not let their youngsters waddle off too far. Danger is always nearby.

If the parents spot a predator, they let out a shrill alarm call. When they hear this sound, the chicks know to scurry under cover—either beneath their parents or into a thicket. They sit motionless until the danger has passed. Their downy feathers are mottled gray. That makes them hard to spot against a background of pebbles, earth, and twigs.

As the chicks get older, they get better at looking after themselves. That gives their parents more time to find enough food for them.

A parent seagull keeps a watchful eye on a brood of chicks.

Two young herring gulls start to find out what life is like without their parents.

Time to Go

From the age of six weeks, the chicks start to grow sleek feathers like the feathers of adult gulls. Those are the feathers they need to fly, and the young gulls are soon up in the air. They do not stray far from the nest, however, because they still need to go home to eat. At this stage, they are still learning to catch food of their own.

After a few more weeks, the chicks are nearly as large as their parents. The young gulls begin to leave the colony and travel to feeding sites. Even if the young gulls cannot catch a lot of food to start with, they can live off the fat they put on when they lived with their parents.

Fun and Games

Life gets easier for gulls as they get older. The young gulls are now such expert hunters that they often get time to take a well-earned rest. In fact, they might even have some energy to spare for some fun and games. Most of the games are used to practice the skills they need to survive. They chase one another through the air, soaring and swooping out of one another's way. They sometimes take turns snatching food from one another's mouth. That will definitely come in handy one day.

A pair of young great black-backed gulls rest on a favorite rock near the ocean.

Soaring high in the air, a gull flies south to warmer parts.

Flying South

Species of gulls that live in the far north find that the weather gets too cold for them in fall. Cold weather is an especially bad problem for gulls that live inland. Their marshes and lakes freeze over, and the surrounding land is covered in deep snow. Their once plentiful supply of fish is no longer accessible. There is only one thing for the gulls to do—fly south.

Some gulls fly almost 1,000 miles (1,600 km) in search of a warmer place to spend winter. The birds travel in small groups. They are strong fliers and can travel at speeds of up to 50 miles (80 km) an hour for days on end. They have a good long rest once they have reached their destination. In spring they fly all the way back home again. Two-way journeys such as those are called **migrations**.

Garbage Hunters

Gulls eat almost anything they can find. They are even happy to eat food offered to them by humans. Often they won't even wait to be offered the food, snatching it off plates or even right out of a person's hand! Gulls pick our beaches and harbors clean, and they are regular visitors to garbage dumps. These birds do such a valuable job of cleaning up after people that they are protected by U.S. law. If the gulls did not eat waste food in garbage dumps, then pests such as rats and cockroaches would move in to take over the job. Gulls are also a great help to many farmers. They eat many of the insects that damage their crops.

Words to Know

Brood　　　　To sit on eggs to keep them warm.

Camouflaged　Blended in with the surroundings.
　　　　　　　　A camouflaged animal is more
　　　　　　　　likely to remain unseen by its
　　　　　　　　predators and prey.

Colonies　　Large groups of gulls living
　　　　　　　　and nesting together.

Down　　　　The soft, fluffy baby feathers
　　　　　　　　that cover newly hatched birds,
　　　　　　　　such as gulls.

Egg tooth　　Toothlike point on the end of a chick's
　　　　　　　　beak used to break out of the egg.

Gland　　　　A body part that releases a certain
　　　　　　　　substance.

Mate　　　　Either member of an animal pair;
　　　　　　　　to come together to produce young.

Migrations Regular two-way journeys in search of food, warmer weather, or a place to raise young.

Molting The process of losing old feathers and growing new ones.

Predators Hunting animals that kill other animals for food.

Preening Cleaning and oiling feathers.

Prey An animal that is hunted for food.

Shellfish Animals such as oysters, crabs, and shrimp that have a hard shell around their body.

Find Out More

Books

DK Publishing. *Bird*. DK Eyewitness Books. New York, New York: DK Publishing Inc., 2004.

Dunn, J. and S. N. G. Howell. *Gulls of the Americas*. Peterson Reference Guides. Boston, Massachusetts: Houghton Mifflin, 2007.

Web sites

Birdguides
www.birdguides.com/html/vidlib/species/Larus_ichthyaetus.htm
Maps and facts about every gull species.

Gull Identification
www.geocities.com/rainforest/canopy/6181/gulls.htm
Photographs and descriptions of gulls; includes quizzes and special features on molting and feathers.

Index